I0781422

Saint Augustine of Hippo:
The Man, The Saint, The Legacy

Saint Augustine, also known as Augustine of Hippo, was a pivotal figure in the history of Christianity. His life, marked by a profound spiritual journey and intellectual exploration, has left an indelible mark on both religious and philosophical thought. Born in North Africa in 354 AD, Augustine's life was characterized by a relentless pursuit of truth and meaning, which ultimately led him to become one of the most influential Christian theologians in history.

Augustine was born in the town of Thagaste, in what is modern-day Algeria. His father, Patricius, was a Roman pagan, while his mother, Monica, was a devout Christian. Augustine's early years were shaped by the tension between his mother's faith and his father's more secular values. Raised in a society that was undergoing a profound transition from paganism to Christianity, young Augustine was exposed to a diverse range of religious and philosophical ideas, which would later play a significant role in his intellectual development.

Augustine displayed exceptional intellectual abilities from a young age. His parents recognized his talent and sought to provide him with the best education possible. He initially studied in Thagaste and then in the nearby city of Madaura. Later, he moved to Carthage to continue his studies, where he was exposed to the teachings of the ancient philosophers, particularly the works of Cicero. Augustine's education instilled in him a love for rhetoric and philosophy, setting the stage for his future endeavors in these fields.

Despite his promising academic career, Augustine's personal life was marked by restlessness. He defied his mother's wishes for him to marry someone from a similar social class, instead embarking on a prolonged love affair that led to the birth of his son, Adeodatus, outside of wedlock. These choices underscored Augustine's divergence from conventional societal norms during his early years, as he wrestled with his own desires and ambitions, ultimately laying the foundation for his later spiritual transformation.

Augustine's spiritual journey took a profound turn when he encountered the Manichean sect, a religious movement that combined elements of Christianity, Buddhism, and Zoroastrianism. He was attracted to the Manichean belief in a dualistic universe of good and evil, as it seemed to provide an intellectual framework that satisfied his philosophical inclinations.

However, his deepening dissatisfaction with the Manichean faith, fueled by growing skepticism, led him on a quest for a more profound and authentic understanding of God. This quest ultimately led him to the teachings of Saint Ambrose, the Bishop of Milan, whose sermons and wisdom had a profound impact on Augustine's thinking. Augustine's encounter with Ambrose marked a turning point in his life, inspiring his eventual conversion to Christianity.

Theological and Philosophical Works

After his conversion to Christianity, Augustine
dedicated himself to a life of intense study and
contemplation. His intellectual journey
culminated in a vast body of writings that have
had a profound and lasting impact on Christian
theology and Western philosophy.

One of Augustine's most renowned works
is his spiritual autobiography, "Confessions."
Written in the form of a prayer, this profound and
introspective text explores his personal journey
from a life of sin and uncertainty to a life
of faith and profound spiritual insight.
In "Confessions," Augustine reflects on the nature
of time, memory, and the relationship between
human beings and God.

Perhaps his most influential work, "The City of
God," was written in response to the fall of Rome
in 410 AD. In this monumental work, Augustine
sought to address the question of theodicy, or the
problem of evil, and to distinguish between the
"City of Man" (the earthly city) and the "City of
God" (the heavenly city). He argued that the true
citizenship of Christians was in the City of God,
and earthly suffering and injustice were
temporary in the grand scheme of divine
providence.

Augustine's theology significantly shaped the
doctrine of original sin. He argued that all
human beings inherit the sin of Adam and are born
with a sinful nature. This concept had a profound
influence on Christian thought and remains a
core doctrine in many Christian traditions.
It's important to note that the idea of

original sin is disputed, with differing interpretations and viewpoints within Christianity.

Augustine was ordained as a priest and later became the Bishop of Hippo (modern-day Annaba, Algeria) in 395 AD. In this role, he provided pastoral care to his community and engaged in theological debates, defending Christian doctrine against various heresies and challenges.

Augustine's works had a profound influence on later theologians, including Thomas Aquinas, Martin Luther, and John Calvin.
His philosophical ideas also played a crucial role in the development of Western philosophy, particularly in the realm of epistemology and the philosophy of mind. His exploration of time, memory, and the nature of God's existence had a significant impact on later philosophers like René Descartes and Immanuel Kant.

Saint Augustine died in 430 AD during the siege of Hippo by the Vandals. Despite the turmoil of his times, his writings and teachings have had a lasting impact on the Christian Church and the broader intellectual world. He was recognized as a Doctor of the Church, and his feast day is celebrated on August 28.

Saint Augustine's enduring legacy continues to inspire and shape the thoughts of theologians, philosophers, and Christians worldwide. His profound exploration of faith, reason, and human nature remains as relevant today as it was in his own time. Augustine's life and work stand as a testament to the transformative power of spirituality and the enduring value of intellectual inquiry.

Major Ideas and Doctrines of Saint Augustine

FREE WILL AND PREDESTINATION: Augustine grappled with the tension between free will and divine predestination. He argued that God's omniscience and sovereignty do not negate human free will. Augustine's perspective was that God, in His divine wisdom, predestines events while still respecting human freedom. This theological standpoint contributed to later discussions about the compatibility of human choice with God's providence, a debate that remains relevant in Christian theology. It raises questions about the balance between divine sovereignty and individual responsibility, inviting continued exploration and debate.

ORIGINAL SIN: Augustine's doctrine of original sin is a foundational concept in Christian theology. He believed that all humans inherit the original sin of Adam, the first human, and are born with a sinful nature. Augustine argued that this inherited sinfulness corrupts human nature and separates individuals from God. This concept has had a profound impact on Christian views of human nature, emphasizing humanity's need for redemption, salvation, and the grace of God. It has also influenced Christian practices such as baptism, which is often seen as a means of cleansing this original sin. However, it's important to note that the doctrine of original sin is not without theological dispute. Over time, Christian theology has evolved, and different traditions have developed their own theological positions on original sin, leading to a diversity of thought on the topic.

THE PROBLEM OF EVIL: In his magnum opus, "The City of God," Augustine delved into the problem of evil, aiming to reconcile the existence of evil and suffering in the world with the presence of an all-powerful and benevolent God. Augustine's perspective on this matter emphasized that evil results from the way in which humans exercise their free will, often through sinful choices and actions. He introduced the concept of the 'City of Man,' representing the fallen, worldly human society, and the 'City of God,' symbolizing the heavenly city of the faithful. Augustine's response to the problem of evil not only laid the foundation for theodicy, the philosophical and theological discipline addressing the existence of evil in a world created by a good and omnipotent God, but also provided a deep theological reflection on the human condition and the consequences of free will.

GRACE AND JUSTIFICATION: Augustine emphasized the importance of divine grace in the process of salvation. He asserted that salvation is a result of God's unmerited favor, and humans cannot achieve it through their own efforts alone. Augustine's emphasis on grace had a significant impact on later theologians, particularly during the Protestant Reformation. Figures like Martin Luther and John Calvin drew on Augustine's ideas when formulating their views on salvation and justification by faith.

TIME AND ETERNITY: Augustine made significant contributions to the philosophy of time and eternity. He introduced the idea that God exists outside of time, an idea that significantly impacted later philosophers and theologians. Augustine's concept challenged traditional understandings of time and the divine, sparking discussions about God's nature, the nature of reality, and the relationship between the temporal and the eternal. This idea influenced later theological and philosophical discussions about divine eternality and the nature of reality.

THEOLOGY OF LOVE: Augustine's theology of love is a central theme in his writings, especially in works like "Confessions" and "On Christian Doctrine." He emphasized that love is the driving force in human existence. Augustine distinguished between earthly or self-love (amor sui) and divine or love of God (amor Dei). He stressed the need for individuals to redirect their love toward God, emphasizing that true fulfillment and purpose can be found in a loving relationship with the divine. Augustine's writings on love continue to influence Christian spirituality and the understanding of the human longing for the divine.

HUMAN NATURE AND THE SELF: Augustine's exploration of human nature and the self is central to his autobiographical work, "Confessions." In this work, he delved into questions of identity, memory, and the relationship between the individual and God. Augustine's introspective examination of his own life and spiritual journey has contributed to the development of introspective and autobiographical literature. His reflections on the nature of the self and the human condition have had a profound influence on both Christian and secular philosophical thought.

RHETORICAL PROWESS: Augustine's early education in rhetoric greatly influenced his later writings and his approach to communicating Christian teachings. He believed that effective communication was vital for conveying the message of Christianity to a wider audience, and his skill in rhetoric allowed him to do so. Augustine's emphasis on eloquence and clarity in expressing theological concepts left a significant mark on Christian rhetoric and preaching, making complex theological ideas more accessible to the general public. However, there are potential negatives to this emphasis as well. Critics argue that a heavy reliance on rhetoric could lead to the manipulation of language for persuasive purposes, potentially detracting from the purity and simplicity of the Christian message. Nevertheless, Augustine's works continue to provide a model for how Christian theology can be communicated effectively, both within the Church and in the broader intellectual and cultural context.

JUST WAR THEORY: Augustine's contributions to just war theory are notable. In his work, "The City of God," he explored the ethical considerations surrounding the use of force and warfare. Augustine argued that a just war could be waged for the sake of defending the innocent and maintaining peace. His ideas have had a lasting impact on the development of the concept of a just war and influenced subsequent discussions on the morality of armed conflict.

SACRAMENTS AND CHURCH AUTHORITY: Augustine's teachings on the sacraments, particularly baptism and the Eucharist, have had a lasting impact on the practices of the Roman Catholic Church. He contributed to the theological understanding of these rituals, emphasizing their importance in the life of the Christian community. Additionally, Augustine played a significant role in defending the authority of the Church against various heresies and schisms. His writings stressed the importance of unity within the Church, which has had a lasting influence on the structure and governance of the Catholic Church.

These are some of the major ideas and philosophies associated with Saint Augustine. His profound and multifaceted contributions continue to shape both Christian theology and Western philosophical thought.

Within the pages of this collection, you will discover the distilled wisdom of Saint Augustine. His eloquent words have resonated through the centuries, offering insights into matters of faith, reason, and the human condition. Let this treasury of Augustine's quotes inspire and enlighten, inviting you to delve deeper into the profound ideas of a saint whose legacy endures as a guiding light in the realms of spirituality and intellectual inquiry.

Let your old age be childlike, and your childhood like old age; that is, so that neither may your wisdom be with pride, nor your humility without wisdom.

Bad times, hard times, this is what people keep saying; but let us live well, and times shall be good. We are the times: Such as we are, such are the times.

Now the Apostle, under
the inspiration of
the Holy Spirit, says,
"Knowledge inflates: but
love edifies." The only
correct interpretation
of this saying is that
knowledge is valuable
when charity informs it.
Without charity,
knowledge inflates; that
is, it exalts man to an
arrogance which is
nothing but a kind of
windy emptiness.

Don't let your life
give evidence
against your tongue.
Sing with your
voices... sing also
with
your conduct.

But it isn't just a matter of faith, but of faith and works. Each is necessary. For the demons also believe — you heard the apostle — and tremble (Jas 2:19); but their believing doesn't do them any good. Faith alone is not enough, unless works too are joined to it: Faith working through love (Gal 5:6), says the apostle.

It is love that asks,
that seeks, that
knocks, that finds,
and that is faithful
to what it finds.

That was an apt and true reply which was given to Alexander the Great by a pirate who had been seized. For when that king had asked the man what he meant by keeping hostile possession of the sea, he answered with bold pride, "What thou meanest by seizing the whole earth; but because I do it with a petty ship, I am called a robber, whilst thou who dost it with a great fleet art styled emperor."

There is, too, a very great difference in the purpose served both by those events which we call adverse and those called prosperous. For the good man is neither uplifted with the good things of time, nor broken by its ills; but the wicked man, because he is corrupted by this world's happiness, feels himself punished by its unhappiness.

Just think of the
illimitable abundance
and the marvelous
loveliness of light, or
of the beauty of the sun
and moon and stars.

Longing desire
prayeth always,
though the tongue be
silent. If thou art
ever longing, thou
art ever praying.

You wish to be great,
begin from the least.
You are thinking to
construct some mighty
fabric in height; first
think of the foundation
of humility. And how
great soever a mass of
building one may wish
and design to place
above it, the greater
the building is to be,
the deeper does he dig
his foundation.

Since you cannot do
good to all, you are to
pay special regard
to those who, by the
accidents of time, or
place, or circumstance,
are brought into closer
connection with you.

For God loves to
save and not to
condemn; therefore
is he patient with
evil, that out of
evil good may be
brought.

On hearing His words let no one say either: "These are not Christ's words," or "These are not my words." On the contrary, if he knows that he is in the body of Christ, let him say: "These are both Christ's words and my words." Say nothing without Him, and He will say nothing without thee. We must not consider ourselves as strangers to Christ, or look upon ourselves as other than Himself.

Understanding is
the reward of faith.
Therefore, seek not
to understand that
you may believe, but
believe that you
may understand.

I held my heart back
from positively
accepting anything,
since I was afraid of
another fall, and in
this condition of
suspense I was being
all the more killed.

Let us leave a little room for reflection in our lives, room too for silence. Let us look within ourselves and see whether there is some delightful hidden place inside where we can be free of noise and argument. Let us hear the Word of God in stillness and perhaps we will then come to understand it.

Whoever thinks that he understands the divine scriptures or any part of them so that it does not build on the double love of God and of our neighbor does not understand it at all. Thus a man supported by faith, hope, and charity, with an unshaken hold upon them does not need the scriptures...

Patience is the
companion of
wisdom.

The punishment of
every disordered
mind is its own
disorder.

There is no love
without hope,
no hope without love,
and neither love nor
hope without faith.

How endlessly futile and
fruitless it would be if
we wanted to refute their
objections every time they
obstinately resolved not
to think through what
they say but merely to
speak, just so long as they
contradict our arguments
in any way they can.

And men go abroad to admire the heights of mountains, the mighty waves of the sea, the broad tides of rivers, the compass of the ocean, and the circuits of the stars, yet pass over the mystery of themselves without a thought.

You have enemies. For
who can live on this
earth without them?
Take heed to
yourselves: love
them. In no way can
your enemy so hurt
you by his violence,
as you hurt yourself
if you love him not.

Grace is given not because we have done good works, but in order that we may be able to do them.

Let us understand
that God is a
physician,
and that suffering
is a medicine for
salvation, not a
punishment for
damnation.

Who is this that cries from the ends of the earth? Who is this one man who reaches to the extremities of the universe? He is one, but that one is unity. He is one, not one in a single place, but the cry of this one man comes from the remotest ends of the earth. But how can this one man cry out from the ends of the earth, unless he be one in all?

For great are you, Lord, and you look kindly on what is humble, but the lofty-minded you regard from afar. Only to those whose hearts are crushed do you draw close. You will not let yourself be found by the proud, nor even by those who in their inquisitive skill count stars or grains of sand, or measure the expanses of heaven, or trace the paths of the planets.

For a sentence is not
complete unless each
word, once its syllables
have been pronounced,
gives way to make room
for the next...They are
set up on the course of
their existence, and
the faster they climb
towards its zenith,
the more they hasten
towards the point where
they exist no more.

A people is an
assemblage of
reasonable beings
bound together by a
common agreement as
to the objects of their
love, then, in order to
discover the character
of any people, we have
only to observe what
they love.

God, grant us men to
see in a small thing
principles which are
common things both
small and great.

Love all men, even your enemies; love them, not because they are your brothers, but that they may become your brothers. Thus you will ever burn with fraternal love, both for him who is already your brother and for your enemy, that he may by loving become your brother. ... Even he that does not as yet believe in Christ ... love him, and love him with fraternal love. He is not yet thy brother, but love him precisely that he may be thy brother.

Let us rejoice and give
thanks. Not only are we
become Christians, but
we are become Christ.
My brothers, do you
understand the grace
of God that is given us?
Wonder, rejoice, for we
are made Christ!

Poverty is the load of
some, and wealth is the
load of others, perhaps
the greater load of the
two. It may weigh them
to perdition. Bear the
load of thy neighbor's
poverty, and let him
bear with thee the load
of thy wealth. Thou
lightenest thy load
by lightening his.

You have been professing yourself reluctant to throw off your load of illusion because truth was uncertain. Well, it is certain now, yet the burden still weighs you down, while other people are given wings on freer shoulders, people who have not worn themselves out with research, nor spent a decade and more reflecting on these questions.

We make a ladder
of our vices, if we
trample those same
vices underfoot.

It is no advantage
to be near
the light
if the eyes
are closed.

Life is a misery, death an uncertainty. Suppose it steals suddenly upon me, in what state shall I leave this world? When can I learn what I have here neglected to learn? Or is it true that death will cut off and put an end to all care and all feeling? This is something to be inquired into.

But no, this cannot be true. It is not for nothing, it is not meaningless that all over the world is displayed the high and towering authority of the Christian faith.

Such great and wonderful things would never have been done for us by God, if the life of the soul were to end with the death of the body. Why then do I delay? Why do I not...devote myself entirely to the search for God and for the happy life?

Sin is to a nature what blindness is to an eye. The blindness of an evil or defect which is a witness to the fact that the eye was created to see the light and, hence, the very lack of sight is the proof that the eye was meant... to be the one particularly capable of seeing the light. Were it not for this capacity, there would be no reason to think of blindness as a misfortune.

You say to me 'Show me your God.' I answer you, 'Everything you see in your heart that might sadden God, remove.'

The past increases by
the diminution of the
future, until by the
consumption of the
future, all is past.

I sought Thee at a
distance, and did not
know that Thou wast
near. I sought Thee
abroad, and behold,
Thou wast within me.

Someone who knows
enough to become the
owner of a tree, and
gives thanks to you for
the benefits it brings
him, is in a better state,
even if ignorant of its
height in feet and the
extent of its spread,
than another who
measures and counts all
its branches but neither
owns it nor knows its
creator nor loves him.

What grace is meant
to do is to help good
people, not to escape
their sufferings, but
to bear them with a
stout heart, with a
fortitude that finds
its strength in faith.

Once for all, then, a short precept is given thee: Love, and do what thou wilt: whether thou hold thy peace, through love hold thy peace; whether thou cry out, through love cry out; whether thou correct, through love correct; whether thou spare, through love do thou spare: let the root of love be within, of this root can nothing spring but what is good.

It is not earthly riches which make us or our sons happy; for they must either be lost by us in our lifetime, or be possessed when we are dead, by whom we know not, or perhaps by whom we would not.

I will plant my feet
on that step where
my parents put me
as a child, until
self-evident truth
comes to light.

You never go away
from us, yet we have
difficulty in
returning to You.
Come, Lord, stir us
up and call us back.
Kindle and seize us.
Be our fire and our
sweetness. Let us
love. Let us run.

The human race is
inquisitive about
other people's lives,
but negligent to
correct their own.

Remove justice, and
what are kingdoms but
gangs of criminals on a
large scale?... A gang
is a group of men... in
which the plunder is
divided according to
an agreed convention.
If this villainy...
acquires territory,
establishes a base,
captures cities and
subdues people, it then
openly arrogates to
itself the title of
kingdom.

Lust indulged
became habit, and
habit unresisted
became necessity.

God became man
so that man
might become God.

Because a thing is
eloquently expressed it
should not be taken to be
as necessarily true; nor
because it is uttered with
stammering lips should it be
supposed false. Nor, again,
is it necessarily true
because rudely uttered, nor
untrue because the language
is brilliant. Wisdom and
folly both are like meats
that are wholesome and
unwholesome, and courtly or
simple words are like town-
made or rustic vessels —
both kinds of food may be
served in either kind
of dish.

It is not the
punishment but
the cause that
makes the martyr.

We must say
something when
those who say the
most are saying
nothing.

Give to the poor.
I beg you, I admonish
you, I charge you, I
command you to give.

A free curiosity is
more effective in
learning than a
rigid discipline.

By faithfulness we
are collected and
wound up into unity
within ourselves,
whereas we had been
scattered abroad
in multiplicity.

Bad company is like a nail driven into a post, which, after the first and second blow, may be drawn out with little difficulty; but being once driven up to the head, the pincers cannot take hold to draw it out, but which can only be done by the destruction of the wood.

Thou must be emptied
of that wherewith
thou art full, that
thou mayest be filled
with that whereof
thou art empty.

O eternal truth and true love and beloved eternity! You are my God; to you I sigh by day and by night. And when I first knew you, you raised me up so that I could see that there was something to see and that I still lacked the ability to see it. And you beat back the weakness of my sight, blazing upon me with your rays, and I trembled in love and in dread...

There is another form
of temptation, more
complex in its peril.
... It originates
in an appetite for
knowledge...Hence do
we proceed to search
out the secret powers
of nature (which is
beside our end), which
to know profits not,
and wherein men desire
nothing but to know.

When I, who conduct
this inquiry, love
something, then three
things are found: I,
what I love, and the
love itself. ... There
are, therefore three
things: the lover, the
beloved and the love.

Remember this.
When people choose to
withdraw far from a fire,
the fire continues to
give warmth, but they
grow cold. When people
choose to withdraw far
from light, the light
continues to be bright in
itself but they are in
darkness. This is also
the case when people
withdraw from God.

Love, and He will
draw near; love,
and He will dwell
within you.

Because God has
made us for
Himself, our
hearts are
restless until
they rest in Him.

For you [God] are infinite and never change. In you 'today' never comes to an end: and yet our 'today' does come to an end in you, because time, as well as everything else, exists in you. If it did not, it would have no means of passing. And since your years never come to an end, for you they are simply 'today'...But you yourself are eternally the same. In your 'today' you will make all that is to exist tomorrow and thereafter, and in your 'today' you have made all that existed yesterday and for ever before.

Beauty grows in you
to the extent that
love grows, because
charity itself is
the soul's beauty.

The members of Christ,
many though they be, are
bound to one another by
the ties of charity and
peace under the one Head,
who is our Saviour
Himself, and form one man.
Often their voice is heard
in the Psalms as the voice
of one man; the cry of one
is as the cry of all, for
all are one in One.

For what is the
self-complacent
man but a slave to
his own self-
praise.

Anger is a weed;
hate is the tree.

Faith is to believe
what you do not see;
the reward of this
faith is to see what
you believe.

And I entered and
beheld with the eye of
my soul... the Light
Unchangeable... He
that knows the Truth,
knows what that Light
is; and he that knows
It, knows Eternity.

The superfluities
of the rich are the
necessaries of the
poor. They who possess
superfluities, possess
the goods of others.

In matters that are so obscure and far beyond our vision, we find in Holy Scripture passages which can be interpreted in very different ways without prejudice to the faith we have received. In such cases, we should not rush in headlong and so firmly take our stand on one side that, if further progress in the search for truth justly undermines this position, we too fall with it.

The moral conscience
is a truly primitive
faculty; it is a
particular manner
of feeling which
corresponds to the
goodness of moral
actions, as taste is
a manner of feeling
which corresponds to
beauty. Love men,
immolate error.

An unjust law
is no law at all.

The confession
of evil works
is the first
beginning of
good works.

Fortitude is the
disposition of soul
which enables us
to despise all
inconveniences and
the loss of things
not in our power.

Walk in your way,
and sing as you walk.
Travelers do this in
order to keep up
their spirits.

For if a thing is not
diminished by being
shared with others,
it is not rightly
owned if it is only
owned and not shared.

The dove loves even
when it attacks;
the wolf hates even
when it flatters.

Wellnigh the whole
substance of the
Christian
discipline
is humility.

As the soul is the life
of the body, so God is
the life of the soul.
As therefore the body
perishes when the
soul leaves it, so the
soul dies when God
departs from it.

How can the past and
future be, when the
past no longer is, and
the future is not yet?
As for the present, if
it were always present
and never moved on to
become the past, it
would not be time,
but eternity.

Beauty is indeed a
good gift of God; but
that the good may not
think it a great good,
God dispenses it even
to the wicked.

No man has a right
to lead such a life
of contemplation as
to forget in his own
ease the service due
to his neighbor.

Just as it is agreed
that we all wish to be
happy, so it is that we
all wish to be wise,
since no one without
wisdom is happy.

The rich are like
beasts of burden,
carrying treasure all
day, and at the night
of death unladen; they
carry to their grave
only the bruises and
marks of their toil.

For it still seemed to me that it is not we who sin, but some other nature sinned in us. And it gratified my pride to be beyond blame, and when I did anything wrong not to have to confess that I had done wrong. ... I loved to excuse my soul and to accuse something else inside me (I knew not what) but which was not I. But, assuredly, it was I, and it was my impiety that had divided me against myself.

A good man, though a
slave, is free; but a
wicked man, though
a king, is a slave.
For he serves, not
one man alone, but
what is worse, as
many masters as
he has vices.

When large numbers
of people share their
joy in common, the
happiness of each is
greater because each
adds fuel to the
other's flame.

The Bible was
composed in such a
way that as beginners
mature, its meaning
grows with them.

Late have I loved you, O Beauty ever
ancient, ever new, late have I loved
you! You were within me, but I was
outside, and it was there that I
searched for you. In my
unloveliness I plunged into the
lovely things which you created.
You were with me, but I was not with
you. Created things kept me from
you; yet if they had not been in you
they would have not been at all. You
called, you shouted, and you broke
through my deafness. You flashed,
you shone, and you dispelled my
blindness. You breathed your
fragrance on me; I drew in breath
and now I pant for you. I have
tasted you, now I hunger and thirst
for more. You touched me, and I
burned for your peace.

What is reprehensible
is that while leading
good lives themselves
and abhorring those
of wicked men, some,
fearing to offend,
shut their eyes to
evil deeds instead of
condemning them and
pointing out their
malice.

I have, however, often
observed this fact of
human behaviour, that
with certain people,
when sexuality is
repressed avarice
seems to grow in
its place.

Though absent from our eyes, Christ our Head is bound to us by love. Since the whole Christ is Head and body, let us so listen to the voice of the Head that we may also hear the body speak.

He no more wished to speak alone than He wished to exist alone, since He says: Behold, I am with you all days, unto the consummation of the world (Matt. 28:20).

If He is with us, then He speaks in us, He speaks of us, and He speaks through us; and we too speak in Him.

Fasting cleanses the
soul, raises the mind,
subjects one's flesh to
the spirit, renders the
heart contrite and
humble, scatters the
clouds of concupiscence,
quenches the fire of
lust, and kindles the
true light of chastity.

The mind commands the
body and is instantly
obeyed. The mind
commands itself and
meets resistance. The
mind commands the hand
to move, and it so easy
that one hardly
distinguishes the order
from its execution. Yet
mind is mind and hand
is body. The mind orders
the mind to will. The
recipient of the order
is itself, yet it does
not perform it.

I was not yet in love,
yet I loved to love...
I sought what I might
love, in love with
loving.

It is not the being
seen of men that is
wrong, but doing
these things for the
purpose of being seen
of men. The problem
with the hypocrite is
his motivation.

What does love look like? It has the hands to help others. It has the feet to hasten to the poor and needy. It has eyes to see misery and want. It has the ears to hear the sighs and sorrows of men. That is what love looks like.

The mind itself, its
love of itself and it
knowledge of itself
are a kind of trinity.

Your first task is to...fight sin, and transform yourself into something better. Your second task is to put up with the trials and temptations of this world that will be brought on by the change in your life and to persevere to the very end in the midst of these things.

How, then, shall I respond to him who asks, "What was God doing before he made heaven and earth?" I do not answer, as a certain one is reported to have done facetiously (shrugging off the force of the question). "He was preparing hell," he said, "for those who pry too deep." It is one thing to see the answer; it is another to laugh at the questioner--and for myself I do not answer these things thus. More willingly would I have answered, "I do not know what I do not know," than cause one who asked a deep question to be ridiculed--and by such tactics gain praise for a worthless answer.

When regard for truth
has been broken down
or even slightly
weakened, all things
will remain doubtful.

By means of corporal
and temporal things
we may comprehend
the eternal and the
spiritual.